WICKED WHEELS

Steve Parker

p

This is a Parragon Book
First published in 2000

Parragon
Queen Street House
4 Queen Street
Bath BA1 1HE, UK

ISBN 0-75253-675-3

Printed in Dubai, U.A.E.

Produced by
Monkey Puzzle Media Ltd
Gissing's Farm
Fressingfield
Suffolk IP21 5SH
UK

Illustrations: Studio Liddell
Designer: Tim Mayer
Cover design: Victoria Webb
Editor: Linda Sonntag
Editorial assistance: Lynda Lines and Jenny Siklós
Indexer: Caroline Hamilton
Project manager: Katie Orchard

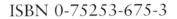

CONTENTS

GETTING AROUND

EARLY WHEELS

Our modern world runs on wheels. But wheels have not always been with us. The first wheels turned around yet lay flat. Potters made bowls and vases on them in the Middle East more than 5,000 years ago. Then some bright spark in Ancient Sumeria had the idea of turning a wheel on its edge and fixing it to a cart. With another three similar wheels at the other three corners, the cart could roll along. This was a great advance on dragging heavy loads. Soon wheels were turning on war chariots, farm wagons and royal coaches.

POWER TO THE PEOPLE

For the next 49 centuries or so wheeled vehicles moved by people or animal power, especially horses and oxen. In the 1800s a human-powered vehicle was developed with two wheels and pedals, which we still use today as the bicycle. Then just over one century ago, in the 1880s, early self-propelled road vehicles appeared. They were powered by new types of engines using liquid fuels. They were developed by German engineers Gottlieb Daimler, Karl Benz and in the 1890s, Rudolf Diesel. These strange. noisy, slow, rattling vehicles were called 'horseless carriages' – a term since shortened to 'car'.

VEHICLES GALORE

Many other road vehicles were soon developed, such as lorries, trucks, public buses, coaches and off-road vehicles, such as jeeps and tractors. Now there are at least 30 main kinds of vehicles on our roads, from bikes and motorcycles to monster trucks and transporters. This book shows many of them, the parts they are made of, how they work and what they and their drivers do.

Speed Bike
With no brakes or gear changers, this bike would be very dangerous on the roads. However, its frame shape and the light-but-strong carbon fibre construction may find their way into the designs of popular mass-produced cycles.

Traffic jam
Perhaps everyone would like to travel in the lap of luxury in their own personal limousine. But traffic jams would be ten times worse than they already are.

ON THE RIGHT TRACKS

The car was not the first engine-driven vehicle. In the early 1800s stationary steam engines were used in mines to pump out water. Wagons with metal wheels that ran on metal rails were also used in mines, pulled by people or ponies to haul coal and rocks. In 1804 Cornish mine engineer, Richard Trevithick, put the two together and made the first mine steam locomotive. In the 1820s George Stephenson made better locomotives to pull a row or 'train' of wagons carrying people, and the railways were born. We still have some steam trains but there are now many other kinds. Some run deep in the subways under cities, others flash through the countryside faster than a racing car.

TAKING TO THE WATER

As steam engines were developed in the 1800s they found their way into ships. No longer did sailors depend on wind. Then petrol, diesel and gas turbine engines were also fitted to ships. Now we have a huge range of ships, boats and other water craft, from racing yachts and powerboats to supertankers.

Intercity to the future?
Super-fast trains whisk people from one city to another at speeds of more than 200 kph (125 mph). The electric locomotives are reliable and cause little pollution. But transport between small villages or hamlets needs more personal and adaptable vehicles than those which carry crowds between the big towns.

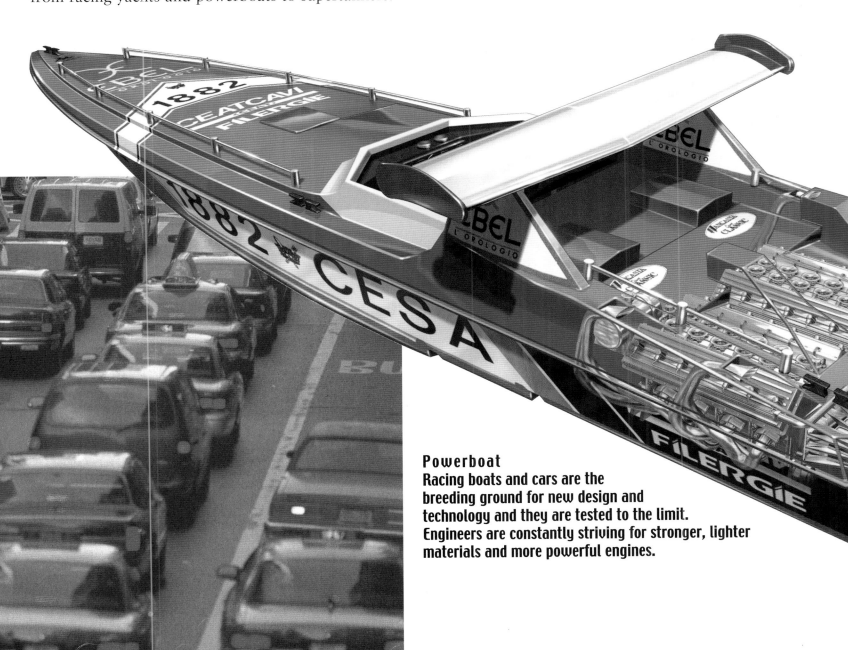

Powerboat
Racing boats and cars are the breeding ground for new design and technology and they are tested to the limit. Engineers are constantly striving for stronger, lighter materials and more powerful engines.

MOUNTAIN BIKE

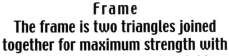

Tread tyres
The tyres have a tread of small, pyramid-shaped blocks. These give good grip on soft ground but they also allow soil or mud to slip off so it does not get stuck and harden in the tread.

Saddle height
The saddle stem tube that holds up the saddle can slide up and down inside the frame's down tube below, so the saddle height can be adjusted.

Frame
The frame is two triangles joined together for maximum strength with minimum materials and weight.

Frame tube
The walls of these tubes are not the same thickness all along. Shallow curves on the inside mean that the tube wall is thinner in the middle, where there is less stress, and thicker at the ends where the most bending strain occurs.

Rear changer
The rear changer has a cage of jockey wheels that moves sideways to shift the chain from one cog to another. This bike has 7 rear cogs, which with the 3 front ones, gives a total of 21 gear combinations.

Front changer
The chain runs through a slot-shaped cage that moves sideways to shift it from one cog to another.

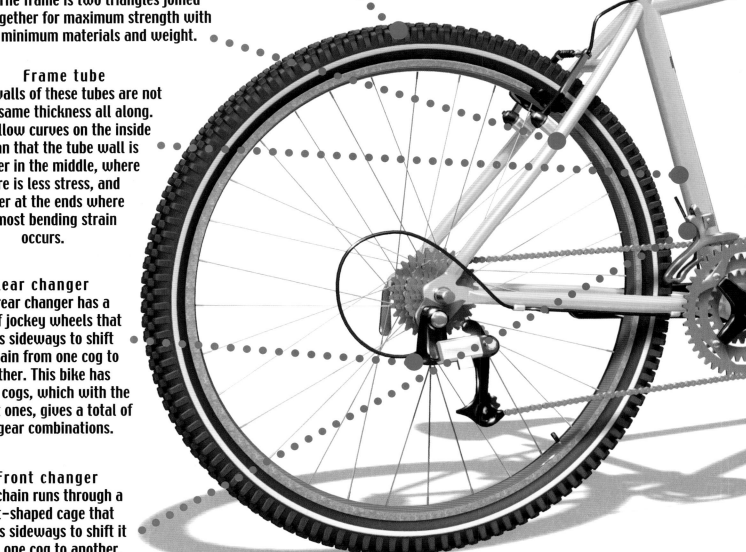

TYPES OF GEARS

Hub gears are contained in an extra-wide rear hub (the central part of the rear wheel). They are changed by a chain that moves in and out of the hub from the side. The chain is worked by a cable attached to a trigger changer on the handlebars. Hub gears usually have only three or perhaps five gear combinations.

Back-pedal gears are also contained in the rear hub. There are two combinations and you change from one to the other by pedalling backwards slightly. In some designs if you back-pedal slightly more you apply the back hub brake.

Derailleur gears as shown here are exposed to rain, mud and grit. But they are easy to clean, adjust and mend and they give the widest variety of gear combinations.

Gear shifts
The gear shift levers or buttons are on the handlebars so the rider can change gear without letting go and losing control.

Safety feature
The handlebars are locked in position by a hex nut (also known as an Allen nut) in the top of their stem. The hex nut has a six-sided hole in it that is turned by inserting a six-sided hex spanner (Allen key). This design means there is no normal nut projecting at the top of the stem. Such a nut could cause injury if the rider slipped and fell on to it.

Handlebar height
The handlebar tube can slide up and down inside the frame tube below, to adjust the height of the handlebars. This is not only for different-sized riders, but also for riding position. Some people like to sit almost upright while others prefer a more crouched posture.

Brake blocks
The brake blocks are made of soft, sticky rubber so that they grip the wheel rim even if it's wet or muddy.

Dampers
The front forks (the two tubes that hold the front wheel) have damper suspension units. One design is a spring to absorb shocks and jolts, plus a pneumatic (air-filled) piston in a cylinder. This restrains the spring's movements so that it does not keep bouncing up and down.

Serrated pedal grip
The pedals have serrated (toothed) edges at the front and back. These stick into the shoe's sole for firm grip.

Quick-release clamp
This type of adjustable clamp is a combination of lever and also nut and bolt. It works fast and you don't need a spanner. You screw the nut by its arm to about half a turn before it gets really tight, then flip over the arm to fully tighten and lock it.

WHY HAVE GEARS?

Imagine a bicycle where you turn the pedals once and the rear wheel turns 10 times. This is a high gear. It's great for speeding downhill where you need little pedalling effort. But you couldn't press the pedals hard enough to turn them when going uphill.

Now imagine a bicycle where you turn the pedals once and the rear wheel turns less than once. This is a low gear. It's great for going up a steep slope, slowly but surely, and with not too much effort. However, you could never turn the pedals fast enough to get up speed when going downhill.

Bicycles have gears for ease and convenience. You can adjust the speed and effort of pedalling to suit you. The bicycle then goes along according to the gearing, usually an average speed on the level, fast downhill or slow uphill. Gears make cycling easier but they don't change the total amount of effort you put in. Low gears make cycling uphill easier. But you are cycling slower and for longer, so your effort lasts longer.

SPEED BIKE

No frame tubes
The frame is one piece of moulded material called carbon fibre composite. It is extremely light and strong, shaped to withstand all the main stresses put on it without any excess material or extra weight.

No freewheel
If you stop pedalling on a sprint or speed bike, the pedals keep turning. There is no freewheel, as on a normal bike, that allows the pedals to stay still while the bicycle rolls along.

ON THE ROAD

Speed bicycles are too specialized to ride on roads. The basic design of the road racer or touring bike, with its down-curved drop-handlebars, has not changed for more than 50 years.

No spokes
As a spoke moves through the air, both turning with the wheel and moving forward with it, this creates air resistance or friction. The solid spokeless wheel cuts out the air friction of the 30–40 normal spokes.

No air-filled tyres
A cycle track is very flat, without lumps and bumps. So the speed or sprint bike needs only thin, solid rubber treads.

No left stays
The back wheel is fixed to one side of the frame, like the front wheel and for the same reason.

No pedal clips
Expert cyclists pull the pedal up as well as push it down, for greater power and speed. Older style pedals had clips and straps that fitted around a cycling shoe. Newer ones have clips that attach to clips on the soles of the shoes, similar to ski bindings that clip ski boots to skis.

BICYCLE SPEEDS

In a road race a cyclist needs air-filled tyres to iron out bumps in the road, gears to cope with the ups and downs of hills and brakes to manoeuvre between competitors or avoid obstacles. But a cycle track is smooth and banked, usually indoors, empty apart from competitors, and exactly the same for every circuit. So the speed or sprint (short race) bicycle is the most stripped-down cycling machine available. Cyclists zoom along at 60 kph (40 mph) or more in races, with top speeds on specially modified cycles of over 100 kph (60 mph).

Elbow rests
The rider rests her or his elbows on these 'shelves' with the forearms lying flat and pointing forwards to grip the handlebars above. The streamlined, torpedo-shaped ends stop the elbows slipping off sideways.

No controls
There are no brakes or gears, so the handlebars look very bare. They face forward so the rider can crouch over them, hands at the front and forearms facing forwards with elbows together. This is the best position for streamlined pedalling.

No gears
The moving parts of gear changers would add friction, weight and wear to the cycle. The sizes of the two gear wheels or cogs, front and back, are chosen by the rider at the start to suit his or her own cycling style, the track, the length of the race, the skill of the competitors and the conditions.

No brakes
There is rarely any need to brake on the special oval, banked cycle track. Brakes merely add more weight and air resistance and get in the way. The pedals can be used to slow the bike down by their fixed drive to the rear wheel.

No left fork
On a normal cycle there are two tubes on either side of the front wheel in a Y shape or fork. The sprint or speed cycle has only one, to cut down air resistance. Like other forward-facing parts it has a narrow leading edge and smooth sides for streamlining.

Not many spokes
The front wheel has three thin spokes. It does not have to be as strong as the rear wheel, which must transmit the turning force from the rear gear cog to the ground, so it can have less construction material.

HIGH GEARS
As you cycle along a level road on an ordinary bike, you push the pedals around once and the back wheel turns around about two times. But sprint and speed cycles have very high gear ratios or combinations. On a speed bike one turn of the pedals turns the back wheel around more – four, five or even more times!

TOURING BIKE

Rear view mirrors
Touring means riding long distances on the open road. Large rear view mirrors are vital for safety, to look behind for overtaking cars and bikes, or for emergency vehicles that need to get past.

Brake lever
This applies the front brake.

Accelerator twist grip
The speed of the engine is controlled by the accelerator twist grip, that is, by twisting the hand grip on the handlebar (usually the right one).

Cooling fins
A car has a cooling system with a radiator to take heat away from the engine. Most motorcycles do not. The cylinder, which is the part that gets hot because the fuel explodes inside it, has many metal flanges or fins. These pass excess heat to the air rushing past.

Fuel tank
The large fuel tank is just in front of the rider. It has a smooth curved top to cause minimum injury in case the rider slips onto it. It may have a map-holder on top, too.

Passenger seat
A second person can travel on the bike, on the second or pillion seat. The passenger should not try to lean or balance the bike. He or she should sit upright, grip the handhold-backrest just behind and act as 'dead weight' to let the rider do the balancing.

Rider's seat
The well-rounded, padded seat is very comfortable for long journeys.

Panniers
A motorcycle has no boot like a car. So luggage is stored in bags or cases called panniers. These are on frames, one on each side of the rear wheel. An equal weight of luggage on either side gives good balance.

Foot rest
The passenger can rest his or her feet on flip-down foot rests that fold back up when not in use.

Rear brake
This is worked by a foot pedal on the right side of the bike. The foot pedal on the other side changes gears.

SPEED AND COMFORT
The freedom of the open road with the wind whistling past, the feeling of being part of the scenery or snaking between cars to beat a traffic jam – motorcycle touring as an 'easy rider' can be great fun. But if it is very cold, raining or icy, it is not so wonderful! The touring bike has a long wheelbase (distance between the wheels) that gives better roadholding and a smoother ride over humps and lumps than a short wheelbase. However, the long wheelbase is not so good for manoeuvring around tight corners.

CYLINDERS AND STROKES

The motorbike shown here is a transverse V twin. It has two cylinders, one each side, at an angle to make a V-shape seen from the front. Two cylinders give a smoother ride and are more powerful than one.

There are many other designs. An in-line twin V has the cylinders one behind the other but still in a V shape seen from the side, one pointing up and forward and the other up and backward. There are also four-cylinder engines that are even smoother and more powerful, but also heavier and more complicated, with more to go wrong.

Many smaller off-road or dirt track motorbikes have just one cylinder. The engine may be a two-stroke. This means that the fuel ignites (explodes) and delivers power every two strokes, that is, every up and down movement of the piston. Normal car and motorcycle engines are four-stroke.

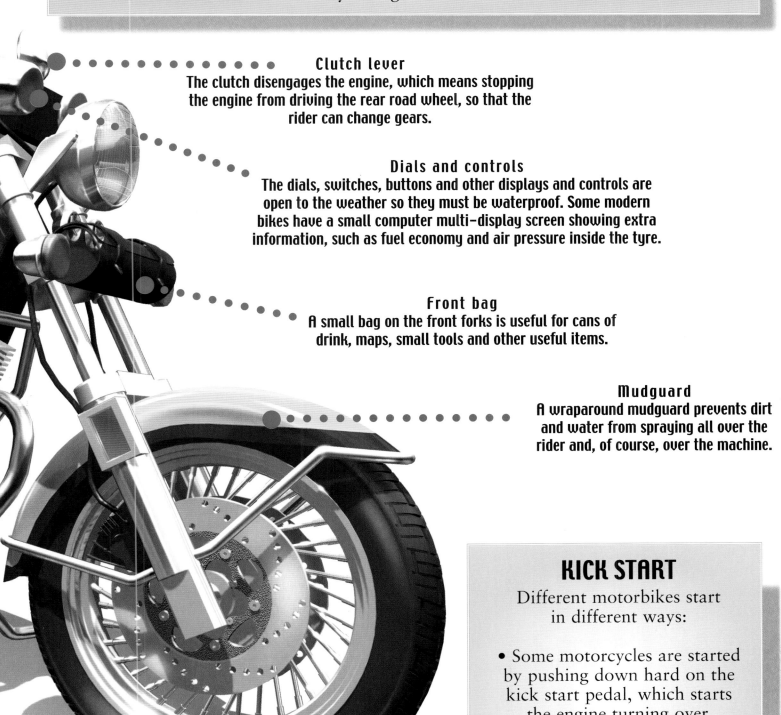

Clutch lever
The clutch disengages the engine, which means stopping the engine from driving the rear road wheel, so that the rider can change gears.

Dials and controls
The dials, switches, buttons and other displays and controls are open to the weather so they must be waterproof. Some modern bikes have a small computer multi–display screen showing extra information, such as fuel economy and air pressure inside the tyre.

Front bag
A small bag on the front forks is useful for cans of drink, maps, small tools and other useful items.

Mudguard
A wraparound mudguard prevents dirt and water from spraying all over the rider and, of course, over the machine.

KICK START

Different motorbikes start in different ways:

• Some motorcycles are started by pushing down hard on the kick start pedal, which starts the engine turning over.

• Others have an electric motor, switched on by turning a key as in a car, to start the engine.

SUPERBIKE

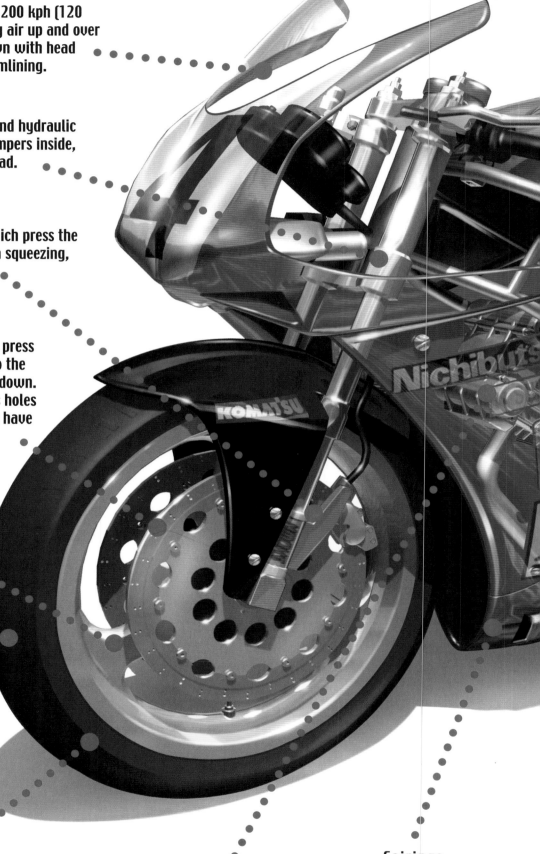

Windshield
The wind is very strong at more than 200 kph (120 mph). The windshield pushes the rushing air up and over the driver, who is also crouched down with head forward into the wind for streamlining.

Front suspension
The front forks are tubes with springs and hydraulic (oil-filled) or pneumatic (air-filled) dampers inside, to smooth out bumps in the road.

Brake calipers
The brake lever works the calipers, which press the brake pads onto the brake disc with a squeezing, scissor-like action.

Brake discs
The brake blocks or pads in the calipers press on to a large metal disc that is fixed to the road wheel and turns with it, to slow it down. The friction makes the disc hot, so it has holes in it for better cooling. Most superbikes have twin discs on the front wheel.

Few spokes
Many modern motorbikes do not have bicycle-type spokes in the wheels. The whole wheel is cast from one piece of metal alloy to make it strong but light. The lighter the wheel, the faster the engine can get it turning.

Slicks
Race tracks and fast roads are usually smooth and free of mud and dirt. So the superbike's tyres, or slicks, do not need tread. They are just plain, soft, sticky rubber to grip the tarmac.

Wraparound
The tyre surface wraps around both sides. This allows the rider to lean over at an amazing angle to balance while going round corners at great speed, with the tyre still gripping the road.

In-line twin V
This engine has two cylinders, one behind the other.

Fairings
A curved plastic or metal cover wraps around the main body of the motorbike to cut down wind resistance.

POWER, WEIGHT AND SPEED

The key to a fast vehicle is its power-to-weight ratio. This compares the weight of the vehicle with the amount of power that its engine produces to drive it along. A superbike might weigh about 170 kilograms (375 pounds) and have an engine that produces 160 horsepower. A family car weighs up to 10 times as much and has an engine that is half as powerful. So its power-to-weight ratio is 20 times less! No wonder superbikes are among the fastest of all vehicles – and so exciting to ride.

Low handlebars
The rider crouches low over the handlebars to minimize wind resistance.

Rider's seat
This is scooped out so that the driver sits as low as possible, hunched over the fuel tank for least wind resistance.

Exhaust
Exhaust gases and fumes from each cylinder flow along pipes that come together into one pipe. They pass through the silencer box before emerging into the air at the back, away from rider and passenger.

Rear suspension
The rear wheel is at the end of a long lever–like arm called a swinging or trailing arm. This pivots with the main chassis just behind the engine. Large springs and hydraulic dampers smooth out bumps and vibrations.

Chain drive
Toothed cogs (sprockets or gear wheels) and a link chain transfer turning power, from the engine between the wheels to the rear wheel. Some bikes have a spinning drive shaft instead of a chain.

Gear pedal
The rider changes gear with a foot pedal by flicking it up and down. The foot pedal on the other side applies the rear brake.

HOW MANY CCS?

A cc is a measure of volume. One cc is one cubic centimetre, that is, a cube roughly the size of a sugar lump. Motorbikes, cars and other vehicles have engines measured in ccs or litres (one litre is 1,000 ccs). The volume that's measured is the amount of air pushed aside as the pistons move their full distance inside their cylinders.

- A small moped or track motorbike is 50 ccs.
- A small racing motorcycle is up to 250 cc.
- A medium motorcycle is 500 ccs.
- A large motorcycle is 750 or 900 ccs.
- There are also superbikes of 1,000 ccs (one litre) and more!
- A smallish family car might have an engine size of 900–1,000 ccs (up to one litre).
- Big luxury cars are 2.5 litres or more.

13

FAMILY CAR

Rear-wheel drive
Most ordinary family cars are rear-wheel drive, where the engine turns only the two roadwheels at the back. This gives the best combination of balance, roadholding, steering and handling. Some smaller cars are front wheel drive, but the extra parts needed both to turn and to steer the front wheels mean extra weight and wear.

Spare wheel and tyre
The spare wheel is usually under one side of the rear of the car next to the fuel tank. If the boot is full, everything must be taken out to change the wheel.

Air bag
In case of a sudden shock or stop, a plastic bag bursts from a container in front of the driver (usually in the middle of the steering wheel) and begins to blow itself up with gas, all in less than one-tenth of a second.

Rear suspension
Springs and hydraulic dampers (pistons in oil-filled cylinders) allow the car body to sway smoothly as the air-filled tyres and the wheels absorb vibrations, bumps and jolts from the road beneath.

Fuel tank
The tank is usually under one side of the rear of the car next to the spare wheel. In this position the fuel is furthest from the hot engine and least likely to catch fire in an accident.

Differential box
This allows the two rear wheels to be turned by the engine at different speeds while going around corners.

CAT
The exhaust fumes and gases are made safer by a CAT or catalytic convertor. This absorbs and keeps back some of the most dangerous exhaust products.

SMART CARS
More and more cars are fitted with electronic gadgets, sensors and microchips. In the engine they monitor how much fuel is being used and help the driver to be more economical. They keep check on the levels of various fluids, such as petrol or diesel fuel, engine oil, gearbox oil, braking system fluid and hydraulic oils, cooling fluid and even windscreen-washer fluid! They also track engine temperature and oil pressure, and warn when replacements will be needed for brakes and other wearing parts.

A satellite navigation unit using the GPS (global positioning system) can pinpoint the car's position to within a few metres on a local map stored in electronic memory, and display this on a screen. Radio and radar links to speed-warning signs tell the driver about exceeding the speed limit. A hands-free mobile phone provides a link to the outside world.

ABS

The automatic braking system (ABS) stops a car from skidding. Without ABS, brakes suddenly jammed on could lock, so the wheels stop turning but the car carries on in a skid. With no grip on the road it's difficult to bring the vehicle to a controlled halt. With ABS, sensors in the wheels react if the brakes are about to lock, and brake pressure is released slightly. This means that the wheel keeps turning and the tyre holds its grip on the road while being slowed down. ABS kicks in several times each second, making a rattling noise. The result is a fast, safe, controlled, non-skid stop.

No sharp corners
Every part of the car's outside is smoothed off for better streamlining and safety. The door handles are recessed or set back into the doors and the rear view or 'wing' mirrors have curved fronts. It all reduces air resistance or drag.

Prop shaft
The engine turns gears in the gearbox and these turn the propeller or prop shaft. It runs along the underside of the car to the differential box between the rear wheels.

Front suspension
This has springs and dampers like the rear suspension. The steering parts are also pivoted so they can tilt as the wheels bob up and down in relation to the engine.

Engine
Most family cars have four-cylinder petrol engines. The modern engine is more than twice as efficient and twice as clean as an engine of 30 years ago. That means it gets twice as much power out of the same amount of fuel and produces only half the amount of harmful exhaust fumes.

Exhaust recycling
Exhaust gases from the engine are sent around again so that the unburned fuel in them can be used more effectively.

Steering mechanism
The steering wheel turns a rod that has a small gear cog or pinion at its base. The teeth of the cog sit in a straight row of teeth known as the rack along another rod, whose ends connect to each front wheel. This is known as rack-and-pinion steering.

WHAT'S THE DIFFERENCE?

The differential allows two wheels on either side of a car to rotate at different speeds while still being driven by the engine. Why? Imagine a car turning left. The wheel on the right covers a longer curve or arc than the left one but during the same time. So it must turn faster to travel the extra distance. If both wheels are being driven at the same speed they lose grip and 'skip' or 'hop' so that they can cover their different distances.

The differential allows this to happen. As the wheel on the outside of the corner turns faster, the one on the inside turns more slowly by the same amount. This gives smooth cornering. Nearly all cars and trucks have this system.

F1 RACING CAR

Front wing
The specially shaped wing produces a force that presses the car down on to the track.

Radio aerial
The driver and his racing team can keep in contact by radio.

Tyre
F1 tyres are wide and have hardly any tread pattern. Tyres for use in the wet have more pattern. During a race, the tyres can heat up to 110 °C.

Wheel
Each wheel is held in place by a single screw-on wheelnut, which can be removed very quickly. This is so that the wheels and tyres can be changed rapidly during a race.

Steering wheel
The small steering wheel is fitted with buttons and switches that enable the driver to change gear and do many other things without having to let go of the wheel.

Cockpit
The driver's cockpit is very cramped, with almost no room to move. It is so small that the driver must remove the steering wheel before he or she gets in or out.

Sponsor's name
Running an F1 racing team is incredibly expensive. Most of the money comes from sponsors, who pay the team to advertize their names on the cars.

Fuel tanks
The tanks on either side of the driver have a honeycomb-like mesh inside. This stops the fuel slopping about too fast inside, which would upset the car's delicate balance.

Driver's survival cell
The driver lies in a tube-shaped survival cell or 'cocoon' made of extremely strong but light composite material, with only the head and arms exposed. The cell resists breaking in a crash to protect the driver.

THE CHAMPIONSHIP MACHINE

The Formula 1 racing car can accelerate from 0–160 kph (0–100 mph) and brake back to a standstill, all in less than six seconds. For this, the driver only needs first and second gears out of the six usually fitted. The fastest speeds are over 320 kph (200 mph). A Formula 1 race is usually about 300 kilometres (nearly 200 miles) and takes up to two hours. Every aspect of the car, including steering angles and fuel tank sizes, is reset for each race track. Dozens of sensors inside the car radio information on every aspect of performance back to the team in the pits. This information transfer is known as telemetry. The team can then advise the driver on the return radio link.

CARS WITH WINGS

Just as the wings of a plane lift it upwards into the air, the wings on an F1 car push it down on to the track. This is because of their shape. On a plane, the top of the wing is curved and the underside is flat, which means that the air presses less on the top than on the bottom, so the wing is pushed upward. F1 car wings are mounted the other way up, so that the force pushes them downwards. This helps the car to grip without slowing it down too much, and gives the driver more control when cornering. The wings and the body shape produce so much force that at 240 kph (150 mph) the car could race upside down on a ceiling and not fall off!

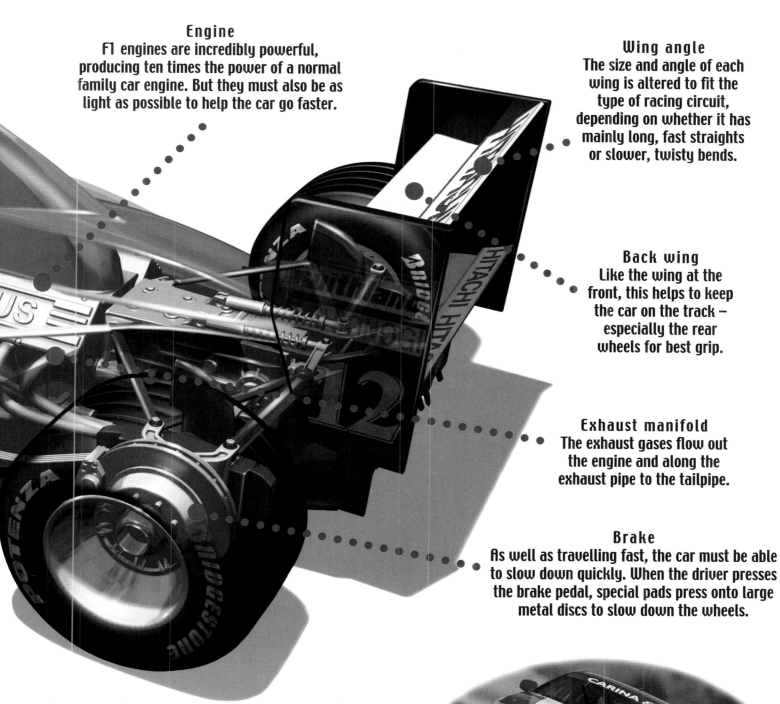

Engine
F1 engines are incredibly powerful, producing ten times the power of a normal family car engine. But they must also be as light as possible to help the car go faster.

Wing angle
The size and angle of each wing is altered to fit the type of racing circuit, depending on whether it has mainly long, fast straights or slower, twisty bends.

Back wing
Like the wing at the front, this helps to keep the car on the track – especially the rear wheels for best grip.

Exhaust manifold
The exhaust gases flow out the engine and along the exhaust pipe to the tailpipe.

Brake
As well as travelling fast, the car must be able to slow down quickly. When the driver presses the brake pedal, special pads press onto large metal discs to slow down the wheels.

TRACK STARS

Many different types of cars race around circuits. As well as Formula One (F1) there are also Formula Two, Formula Three and smaller formulas. Rally and touring cars (right) look more like normal family cars – but they too go much, much faster!

STRETCH LIMOUSINE

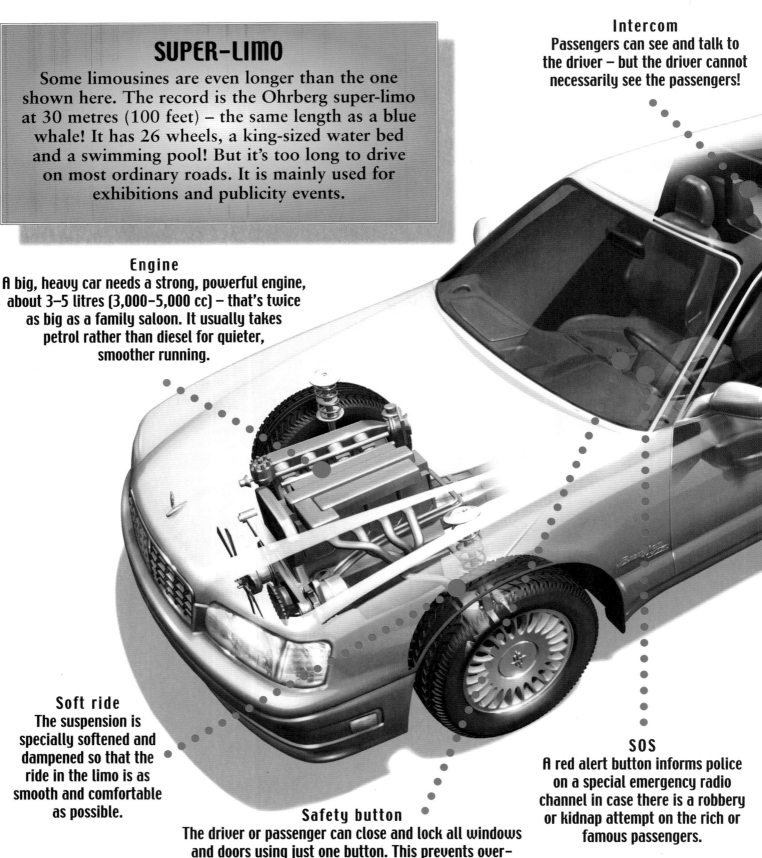

SUPER-LIMO

Some limousines are even longer than the one shown here. The record is the Ohrberg super-limo at 30 metres (100 feet) – the same length as a blue whale! It has 26 wheels, a king-sized water bed and a swimming pool! But it's too long to drive on most ordinary roads. It is mainly used for exhibitions and publicity events.

Intercom
Passengers can see and talk to the driver – but the driver cannot necessarily see the passengers!

Engine
A big, heavy car needs a strong, powerful engine, about 3–5 litres (3,000–5,000 cc) – that's twice as big as a family saloon. It usually takes petrol rather than diesel for quieter, smoother running.

Soft ride
The suspension is specially softened and dampened so that the ride in the limo is as smooth and comfortable as possible.

Safety button
The driver or passenger can close and lock all windows and doors using just one button. This prevents over-keen fans or curious sightseers from getting into the car.

SOS
A red alert button informs police on a special emergency radio channel in case there is a robbery or kidnap attempt on the rich or famous passengers.

THE STRETCHED PART

Originally the 'stretch' limousine was made by taking an existing luxury car, cutting it in half and welding extra panels into the gaps to make it longer. Then a new top-class interior was fitted with leather seats, deep-pile carpets and all the trimmings. Today, various specialized vehicle-makers build limos exactly to the owner's wishes. Some have fold-out beds so that they can become a luxury hotel on wheels!

Mobile office
On long journeys the limo can be a place to work. It may be fitted with a computer linked to the Internet, and a video player so that movie or music star passengers can view their latest scenes.

Radio links
Various aerials and antennae send and receive signals for radio, TV, telephone, Internet and also private encrypted (secrecy-coded) radio and walkie-talkie channels.

Tinted windows
The windows to the passenger compartment are tinted and have a reflective coating. People trying to see in from the outside can only see their own faces. The windows are often bullet-proof, too.

Comforts of home
The limo has a mobile phone, a TV (terrestrial and satellite of course), a stereo system, a courtesy bar, hot drinks and many other comforts.

Expert driver
The driver or chauffeur must be specially trained not only to drive safely and within the law, but also to start and stop very smoothly and to guide the long limo around awkward turns and avoid too-sharp corners.

Keeping cool and quiet
Air conditioning keeps passengers warm in cold weather or cool when it is hot. It also filters out the smoke and fumes from traffic jams. Special body panels and thick windows keep out the noise.

WHO BUYS A STRETCH LIMO?

Whoever wants one and has enough money! However, it is a very expensive 'toy' to leave sitting in the garage. And it may not get through the barrier at the local supermarket car park. This is why 19 out of 20 large limousines are owned by vehicle hire companies. A limo can be rented by the hour, day, week or longer. The driver costs money, too. Big limos are hired for film and music stars, bosses of big companies, royalty, presidents and prime ministers, important politicians and public figures. And also the ordinary family who decide to splash out on a special day, such as a wedding or anniversary.

4WD - FOUR WHEEL DRIVE

Silencer
This box in the exhaust pipe makes the waste gases and fumes from the engine slower and quieter. It may also contain a CAT (catalytic convertor) with special substances that remove some of the most dangerous chemicals in the fumes.

ATTs
All terrain tyres have thicker, chunkier tread than normal road tyres. They give good all-purpose grip on a variety of surfaces, from motorways to ploughed fields.

Chassis
Steel box girders make the car's chassis or framework very strong and rigid, so that it can withstand knocks from rocks and potholes.

Rear door
Some rear doors are hinged to the roof so they lift up in one piece. Others are horizontal two-part so the window section folds up and the lower solid part hinges down to form a tailgate platform. Still others are vertical two-part, hinged at each side so they open in the middle.

Rear drive
The rear drive or half shafts turn the rear road wheels when the vehicle is in RWD or 4WD mode.

Light cages
If a 4WD is used off-road it may skid and bump into trees, posts and other objects. Wire cages around the lights prevent their coverings and bulbs from being smashed. It's easier to straighten out the wire cage than to replace the bulb and cover.

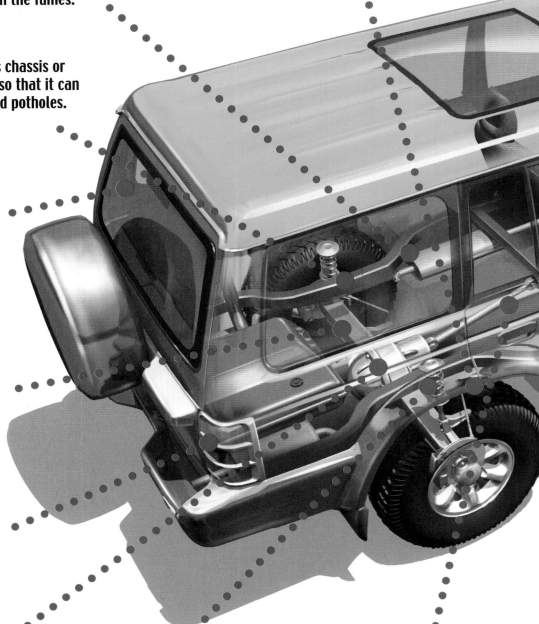

Limited slip diff
This box of gear cogs stops the vehicle from getting bogged down in slippery mud.

Suspension
4WDs have strong, stiff suspension to cope with bumps and lumps on rough ground and also with the heavy loads they may carry.

Prop shaft
The propeller shaft carries the turning force from the engine back to the rear road wheels.

WHY 4WD?

A normal family car is 2WD or two wheel drive – only two of the road wheels are turned by the engine. In small cars it may be the front two (FWD), in larger ones it's the rear two (RWD). In a 4WD (four-wheel drive) vehicle all four road wheels are made to turn by the engine. This allows much more power to get through to the road, giving improved grip or traction. The vehicle has a better grip on slippery mud and ice. There is more control in going up and down very steep hills and getting out of potholes or over rocks and roots. It also allows heavier loads to be carried.

However, 4WD uses up much more fuel. This is because the engine has to turn and work an extra set of road wheel drive parts. So most 4WDs have a lever or button that switches to 2WD for smooth roads, to save fuel and wear and tear.

Head restraint
As a 4WD travels over rough ground the passengers bump and sway about. Shaped restraints help to steady their heads so that they can avoid neck pain and whiplash injuries.

Engine
Most 4WDs have diesel engines. They may be heavier and noisier than petrol engines, but they are usually more reliable and also need less servicing and maintenance.

Drive control
The driver uses a lever or shiftstick to change between FWD, RWD and 4WD.

Front drive
The front drive shafts turn the front road wheels when the vehicle is in FWD or 4WD mode.

Disc brakes
A big, heavy car like a 4WD needs strong brakes, so it is fitted with disc brakes all around. These are power–assisted, which means that the driver's pressure on the foot pedal is greatly boosted by hydraulic pressure supplied by the engine.

EVEN MORE GRIP

Four wheels turning may not be enough in very slippery conditions like ice and snow. So special snow chains are wrapped around the tyres to give even more 'purchase' (grip).

LIMITED SLIP DIFF

In a 2WD vehicle, the wheels on either side of the axle can rotate at different speeds while still being driven by the engine. This is called the diff or differential. But it can cause trouble when off road. Imagine the left back wheel of the car is in a very slippery place such as on ice. It has hardly anything to grip, so it can spin almost freely. The diff allows it to do this, while the right back wheel – which is on dry tarmac and can grip – simply stays still. The vehicle is stuck! This doesn't happen when a vehicle has limited or non-slip diff. Only a limited difference is allowed between the speeds of the two wheels. Beyond this the drive is still applied to the slower wheel, which hauls the vehicle out of the rut, so it's no longer stuck.

PICK-UP TRUCK

Turbo diesel
The turbocharged diesel engine has about twice the power of an ordinary family car engine.

Winch
This is a cable wound on to a reel or drum, with a hook or link on the end. The drum spins easily one way so that the cable can be unwound. Then the drum turns slowly but powerfully to wind it back in. If the pick-up is parked, the winch can haul items towards it. If the pick-up cannot climb a steep hill, the cable can be unwound and attached to something higher up, such as a tree, pole or building. Then the winch turns to pull up the pick-up!

Bull bar
There aren't usually many real bulls to push out of the way. The bull bar is really a large front fender for pushing branches and other items aside or to protect the pick-up in case of a crash.

Clean headlamps
Because pick-ups often travel over soft ground and unmade roads, they get covered in mud. The headlamps have their own water sprayers and wipers to keep them clean.

Stiff suspension
The pick-up's suspension springs and dampers are very stiff. That is, they do not soften the ride very much. This is because pick-ups are built to carry heavy loads over rough grounds, where soft suspension might strain or break.

Ground clearance
All parts on the underside of the pick-up are well above the ground. This is called high ground clearance and prevents damage as the vehicle goes over rocks and roots. There may be sheets of metal, under-pans, covering the undersides of more fragile parts.

4WD
Most pick-ups have four-wheel drive where the engine turns all four road wheels.

MANY JOBS IN ONE

The combine harvester is named after the fact that it combines or joins together all the jobs normally done when harvesting grain crops, such as wheat, barley, oats and rye. The first combines appeared in the USA in the 1920s, towed and powered by tractors. Self-propelled combines with their own engines became popular in the 1950s. Modern combines have a range of cutting heads, bars and reels to suit different crops, including beans, sweetcorn and sorghum. Each one does the work of up to 100 people using hand-harvesting tools.

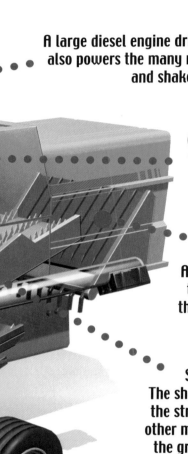

Engine
A large diesel engine drives the combine's main wheels and also powers the many moving parts, belts, screws, augers and shakers inside the vehicle.

Grain tank
Grain is stored here until the tank is full, or it can be blown or conveyed into a truck or trailer that is driven alongside the combine as it crawls across the field.

Baler
A baling attachment can be fitted to the rear of the combine. It presses the straw into box-shaped bales and ties them with twine.

Straw walker or shaker
The shaker rattles to and fro and shakes the straw (stalks) rearwards. Grain and other material fall through the sieve onto the grain pan. Another corkscrew-like auger lifts the threshed, clean grains up into the main storage tank.

Grain pan
The grain is carried backwards and powerful blasts of air from the chaff fan blow the lighter unwanted bits and pieces (chaff) upwards away from it.

Drive wheels
The large wheels under the main part of the machine push the combine along. Smaller wheels at the rear steer the vehicle.

Threshing cylinder
The thresher turns around and shakes the crop so violently that the seeds (grain) fall away from the seed cases, stalks, leaves and other unwanted bits.

COMPUTERIZED COMBINES

Remote sensing satellites far above in space can survey huge expanses of fields that would take a long time to check on the ground. The satellites beam pictures of the fields down by radio. The farmer can tell by the different computer-enhanced colours which areas of crop may be diseased or in need of pesticides, fertilizers or other sprays and which are ready to harvest. This information, plus the size and shape of the area to be cut, are fed into the combine's on-board computer.
The computer works out the best route for harvesting the field. It can also avoid any poor areas that are not worth cutting. The route is displayed on a screen for the driver to follow.

DIGGER

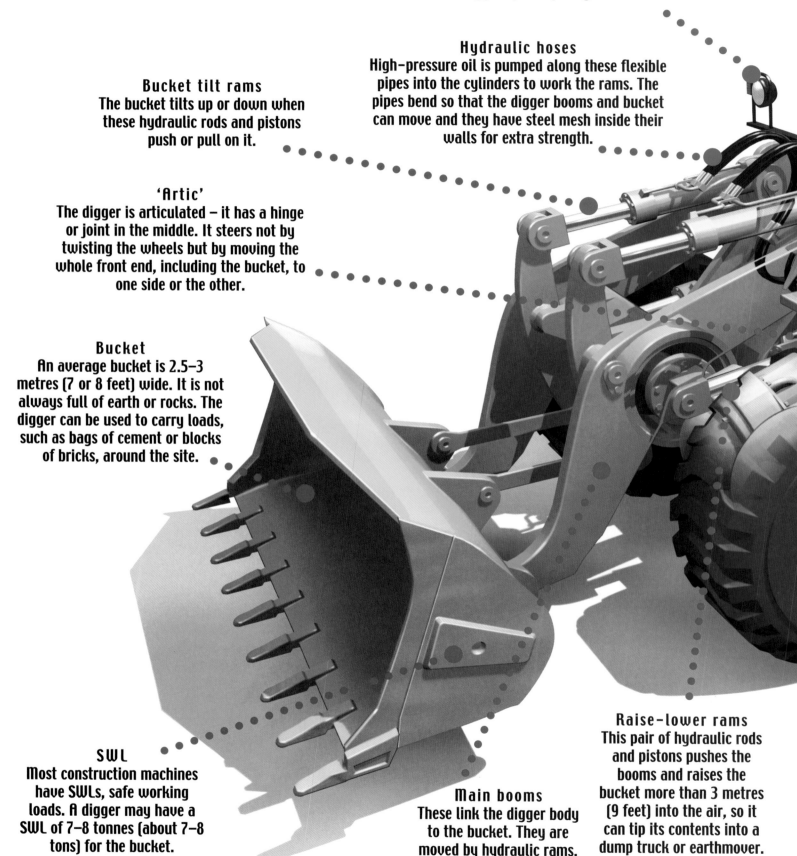

Lights
To get the job done on time the digger and driver may have to work nights. The lights move with the bucket so it is always brightly lit. There are also lights at the rear, and the driver's seat swivels round, too, since a digger spends plenty of time in reverse.

Hydraulic hoses
High-pressure oil is pumped along these flexible pipes into the cylinders to work the rams. The pipes bend so that the digger booms and bucket can move and they have steel mesh inside their walls for extra strength.

Bucket tilt rams
The bucket tilts up or down when these hydraulic rods and pistons push or pull on it.

'Artic'
The digger is articulated – it has a hinge or joint in the middle. It steers not by twisting the wheels but by moving the whole front end, including the bucket, to one side or the other.

Bucket
An average bucket is 2.5–3 metres (7 or 8 feet) wide. It is not always full of earth or rocks. The digger can be used to carry loads, such as bags of cement or blocks of bricks, around the site.

SWL
Most construction machines have SWLs, safe working loads. A digger may have a SWL of 7–8 tonnes (about 7–8 tons) for the bucket.

Main booms
These link the digger body to the bucket. They are moved by hydraulic rams.

Raise-lower rams
This pair of hydraulic rods and pistons pushes the booms and raises the bucket more than 3 metres (9 feet) into the air, so it can tip its contents into a dump truck or earthmover.

BUCKETS OF BUCKETS

The bucket shown here is a typical all-purpose design for gouging into and lifting soil, earth, small rocks, shingle, gravel and sand. There are many other bucket designs for different jobs. A smoothing bucket is lower and wider to scrape a large area level. A basket bucket is made of steel bars like a cage for lifting lighter, looser material such as hay, straw and household refuse.

Cab
The driver sits in an air-conditioned, vibration-proofed and sound-proofed cab. This protects the driver from being deafened and shaken up by a day's work.

Controls
Hand levers or buttons control the bucket's movements. Floor pedals and the steering wheel make the whole digger move about.

Engine
A heavy-duty diesel engine provides the power for turning the wheels and for the hydraulic system to raise and lower the bucket. The engine produces about 180–200 horsepower (almost three times the power of a smallish family car engine).

Massive tyres
A big digger has tyres taller than an adult person. They have deep tread to grip soft ground. Sometimes they are filled partly with water for extra weight and grip.

DIGGERS GALORE
Diggers, excavators and other load-movers find jobs in all kinds of work, from piling up scrapped cars, to scooping up gravel and sand for building, to scraping up sea salt from shallow coastal lagoons.

IT'S ALL DONE BY HYDRAULICS
Many large vehicles and machines rely on hydraulic systems. They use oil under very high pressure. It is pumped along a pipe or hose into a large metal tube-shaped cylinder. Closely fitting inside the cylinder is a rod-shaped piston. As the oil is forced into the cylinder it pushes the piston in front of it. The piston usually has a long metal rod fixed to it and the other end of the rod is linked to the part that moves. The pressure is so great that if a hose sprang a leak, the thin jet of oil spurting out of it would blast a small hole straight through the body of a person standing in the way.

Like our own muscles, hydraulic pistons can only push. For two-way movement there are two pistons that rock the part to be moved like a see-saw. Or two pistons face each other in the same long cylinder and the oil is pumped from one end of the cylinder to the other. This gives push-pull power.

BULLDOZER

Blade controls
These levers control the hydraulic rams to raise or lower the blade and to tilt it up or down.

Dozer controls
There are very few controls for the bulldozer itself. The main ones are two levers that make the tracks work on each side. The dozer has no steering wheel. It turns by slowing or stopping the track on one side while the other track still runs, making the dozer swing or pivot around at its middle.

Track drive
The main cog or sprocket wheel is driven by the engine to make the track run. On some dozers there is a front drive cog, too, and perhaps repeater cogs along the length of the track.

Track
The track is the caterpillar or crawler track, an endless loop of plates joined by pins.

Hydraulic array
The engine supplies the main hydraulic power to the cab, in the form of oil at very high pressure in a pipe. This is divided into many pipes, each with its own control, that send oil to work the various hydraulic rams and systems.

Track pin
Pins link the track plates to each other. If one plate gets bent or broken, the pins can be taken out and a new plate inserted.

Track plate
Some tracks have plates made of very hard and strong rubber, others of metal. The ridge across the track jabs into the ground to give amazing grip.

WHY THE NAME?
The name is a version of the term 'bull dose'. This was a dose of sedative given to a bull, which was more powerful than that needed by a smaller, calmer cow. So giving a 'dose fit for a bull' meant giving an extra-powerful or very strong amount of something. It suited the bulldozer's great size and mighty power.

WHAT DO BULLDOZERS DO?

They are designed to push, scrape and level rough ground and to move piles of rocks, earth, gravel, sand and other loose material. But they can do much more:

- A bulldozer can drive through an area of scrub, young trees or rough ground, flattening everything in its path.

- It can attach a cable or chain to bigger trees and pull them out of the ground, or drag over walls and pylons.

- Two bulldozers with a long steel cable or hawser strung between them can drive either side of a wood or old weak building and make it topple to the ground.

- A bulldozer can also push and move heavy items, such as large steel pipes.

- The bulldozer can rescue other vehicles if they get stuck by dragging them out of ruts or mud on to solid ground.

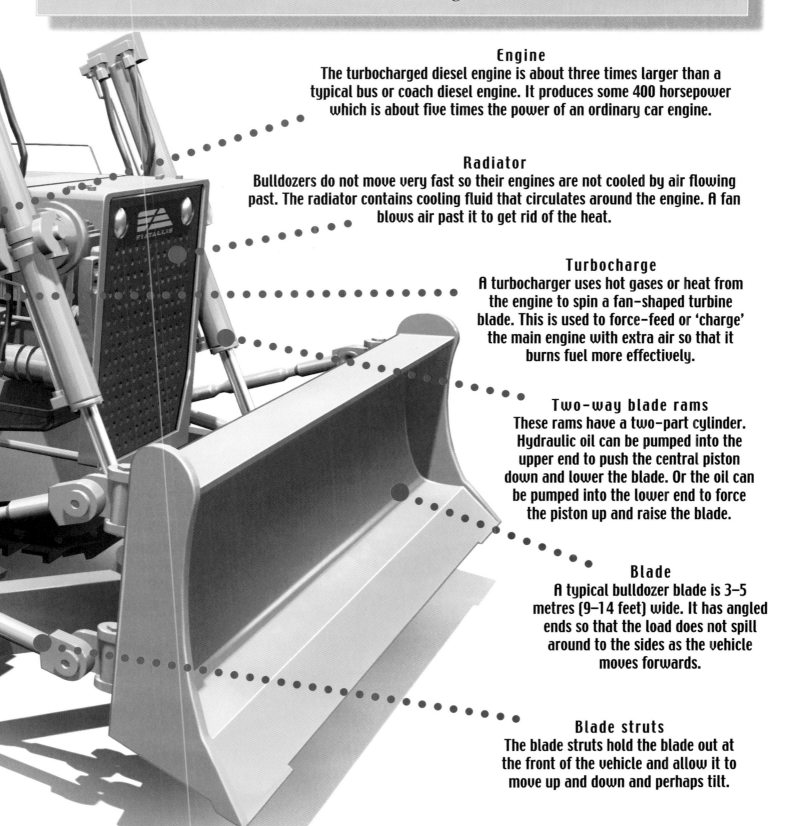

Engine
The turbocharged diesel engine is about three times larger than a typical bus or coach diesel engine. It produces some 400 horsepower which is about five times the power of an ordinary car engine.

Radiator
Bulldozers do not move very fast so their engines are not cooled by air flowing past. The radiator contains cooling fluid that circulates around the engine. A fan blows air past it to get rid of the heat.

Turbocharge
A turbocharger uses hot gases or heat from the engine to spin a fan-shaped turbine blade. This is used to force-feed or 'charge' the main engine with extra air so that it burns fuel more effectively.

Two-way blade rams
These rams have a two-part cylinder. Hydraulic oil can be pumped into the upper end to push the central piston down and lower the blade. Or the oil can be pumped into the lower end to force the piston up and raise the blade.

Blade
A typical bulldozer blade is 3–5 metres (9–14 feet) wide. It has angled ends so that the load does not spill around to the sides as the vehicle moves forwards.

Blade struts
The blade struts hold the blade out at the front of the vehicle and allow it to move up and down and perhaps tilt.

MONSTER TRUCK

Cockpit
There are lots of extra dials and controls in the cab, because many running conditions of the highly tuned engine, such as temperatures and pressures, must be closely monitored. The dashboard looks more like a plane cockpit or flight deck.

Air horns
Compressed air blasts out of the multi-horns to make a sound heard more than 2 kilometres (1 mile) away.

CB radio
Drivers keep in touch with each other by CB or citizen's band radio. They chat and pass the time of day, discuss the weather and road conditions, or their trucks and loads, and warn each other of traffic jams or accidents.

Limiter
Working trucks are fitted with speed limiters since in many countries they are not allowed to go as fast as ordinary cars.

Gears
There may be 10, 12 or more gears to help the truck pull away uphill with its 40-tonne load or cruise down the motorway at its maximum speed.

Driver's seat
The driver's seat is reinforced and strengthened, with a pilot-like safety harness for a seat belt, to cope with the tremendous acceleration and cornering speed.

Engine
The giant turbocharged diesel engine may be 10 times the size of a family car engine. Some speed trucks are even fitted with jet engines as used on fighter aircraft!

Square shape
This truck has few curves. Its design is flat-sided and squared-off. This makes it look strong and powerful. But it is not so good for speed and fuel economy.

Shiny chrome
On a show truck such as this many of the parts are coated with chrome metal for a shiny, hard-wearing appearance. But that means a lot of polish to keep the vehicle looking clean!

HOW MANY RAILS?

The subway shown here has four rails. The train runs on two. The electricity comes in along a live current rail on one side, and is carried away along the neutral current rail on the other side. Other designs have just one live current rail, called the 'third rail'. They use the running rails to carry the electricity away again.

Every section of track has sensors that monitor how much electricity is passing along the rails. If there is a sudden surge, perhaps due to an accident, the current is switched off within a fraction of a second.

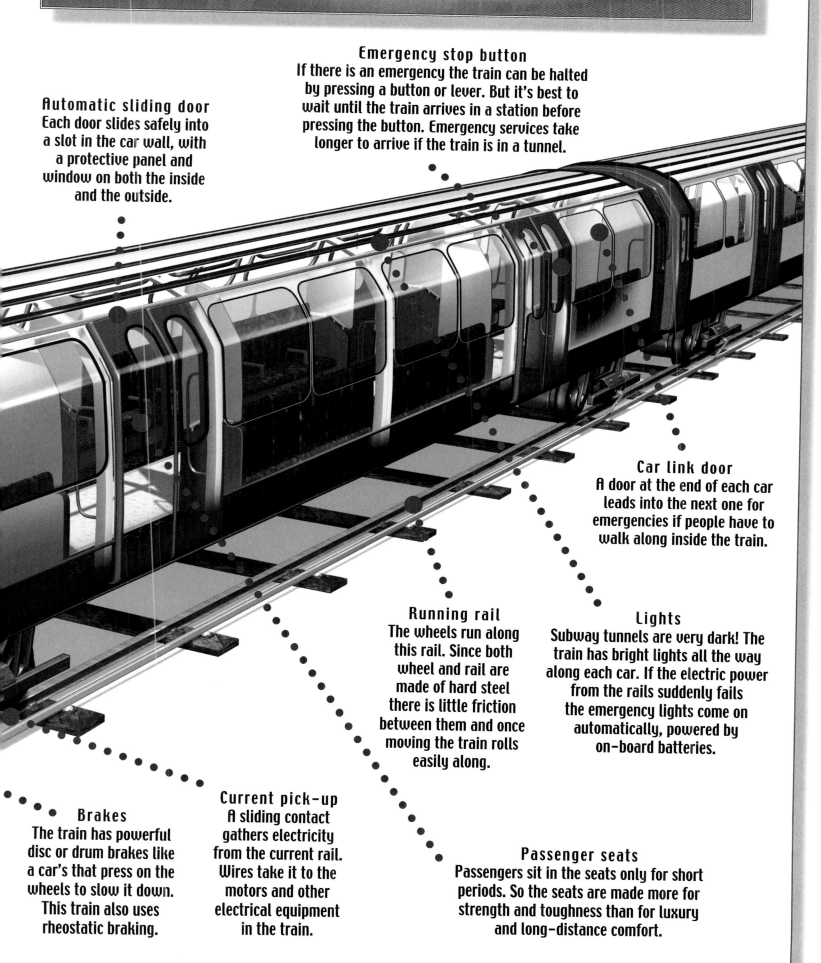

Emergency stop button
If there is an emergency the train can be halted by pressing a button or lever. But it's best to wait until the train arrives in a station before pressing the button. Emergency services take longer to arrive if the train is in a tunnel.

Automatic sliding door
Each door slides safely into a slot in the car wall, with a protective panel and window on both the inside and the outside.

Car link door
A door at the end of each car leads into the next one for emergencies if people have to walk along inside the train.

Running rail
The wheels run along this rail. Since both wheel and rail are made of hard steel there is little friction between them and once moving the train rolls easily along.

Lights
Subway tunnels are very dark! The train has bright lights all the way along each car. If the electric power from the rails suddenly fails the emergency lights come on automatically, powered by on-board batteries.

Brakes
The train has powerful disc or drum brakes like a car's that press on the wheels to slow it down. This train also uses rheostatic braking.

Current pick-up
A sliding contact gathers electricity from the current rail. Wires take it to the motors and other electrical equipment in the train.

Passenger seats
Passengers sit in the seats only for short periods. So the seats are made more for strength and toughness than for luxury and long-distance comfort.

OFFSHORE POWERBOAT

Cockpit
The driver and co-driver sit in the cockpit with an array of dials, switches, buttons and screens in front of them. They rely on these instruments because the waves and spray mean they can often see little.

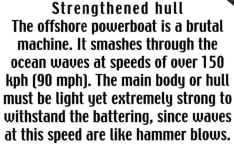

Strengthened hull
The offshore powerboat is a brutal machine. It smashes through the ocean waves at speeds of over 150 kph (90 mph). The main body or hull must be light yet extremely strong to withstand the battering, since waves at this speed are like hammer blows. The hull is usually made of aluminium or carbon fibre composite.

Spray rail
This lip or shelf along the hull pushes most of the spray and water aside so it does not break over the boat itself.

THE RACE
Powerboat races may be around a marked-out course or across the open sea from one town or island to another. This type of racing looks glamorous but it is very tiring and stressful.

SAFETY FIRST
Speeding powerboats don't lie in the water and push it aside. They plane or skim over the surface. Only the very rear parts with the screws and rudders dip into the water. However, the boat can't avoid tall waves, and these produce huge shocks as they hit. For this reason the crew must be fit and tough. The driver steers the powerboat, using satellite navigation and many other electronic aids. The co-driver controls the speed of the engines using their throttles and adjusts the boat's trim. Both crew are attached to a 'kill switch' by long cords. If they are accidentally thrown out of their seats the kill switch stops the engine so that the powerboat does not race away out of control across the sea.

F1 BOATS

Offshore powerboats have incredible strength and power for racing across the open sea. And just as Formula One is the top level for racing cars around a special track, Formula One powerboats (smaller than the boat shown here) are the top level on water. They race in sheltered waters around marker buoys, following a course similar to a Formula 1 car circuit, for 50–60 laps. They are small and streamlined catamarans – two long, slim hulls side by side under the main body. F1 boats have outboard engines, fixed on by a hinged bracket at the back. They can reach speeds of more than 250 kph (150 mph).

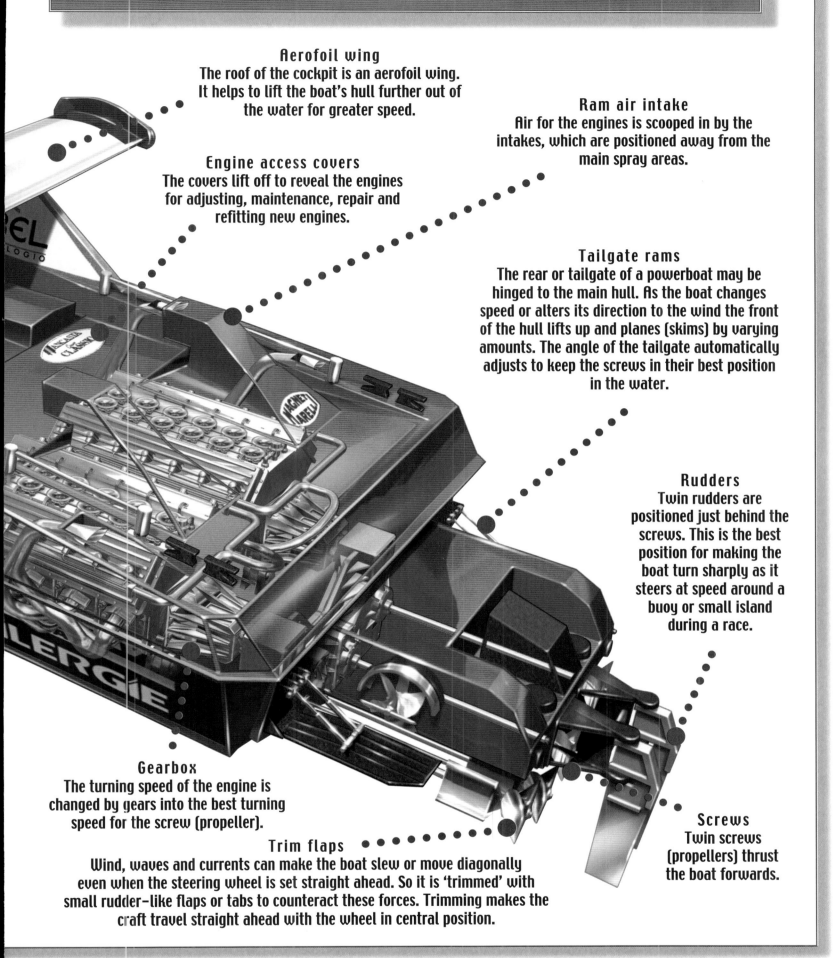

Aerofoil wing
The roof of the cockpit is an aerofoil wing. It helps to lift the boat's hull further out of the water for greater speed.

Ram air intake
Air for the engines is scooped in by the intakes, which are positioned away from the main spray areas.

Engine access covers
The covers lift off to reveal the engines for adjusting, maintenance, repair and refitting new engines.

Tailgate rams
The rear or tailgate of a powerboat may be hinged to the main hull. As the boat changes speed or alters its direction to the wind the front of the hull lifts up and planes (skims) by varying amounts. The angle of the tailgate automatically adjusts to keep the screws in their best position in the water.

Rudders
Twin rudders are positioned just behind the screws. This is the best position for making the boat turn sharply as it steers at speed around a buoy or small island during a race.

Gearbox
The turning speed of the engine is changed by gears into the best turning speed for the screw (propeller).

Screws
Twin screws (propellers) thrust the boat forwards.

Trim flaps
Wind, waves and currents can make the boat slew or move diagonally even when the steering wheel is set straight ahead. So it is 'trimmed' with small rudder-like flaps or tabs to counteract these forces. Trimming makes the craft travel straight ahead with the wheel in central position.

sleeping quarters.

also a table with maps and charts laid out for navigation.

the position of the sails and how the wind blows at them.

Auxiliary power
Most yachts have a small engine that turns a screw to drive the craft slowly along. This is useful not only when there is a flat calm, but also for manoeuvring between other boats and when tying up in a port.

Keel
The large flange or keel sticking down from the bottom of the hull stops the yacht from capsizing. It also helps to keep the yacht moving in a straight line as it leans with the wind.

Rudder
The wheel controls the rudder, making it swing left or right to steer the yacht.

RACING YACHT

mast

SUPERTANKER

THE GIANT IN PORT

Supertankers are so vast and awkward to manoeuvre that they do not come into small harbours. Large terminals are built for them where there is plenty of room and the water is deeper. Small, powerful tug boats push them into position.

Crew gangway
Crew members can quickly reach any part of the deck along the gangways. Often they use bicycles, since the whole ship may be more than 300 metres (800 feet) long.

Pipes
A maze of pipes connects the various tanks and pumps with the connectors for loading or unloading the oil.

Pumps
Various pumps force the oil into the tanks when loading at the oil production platform. They suck it out again when the supertanker reaches its destination – the oil refinery or storage depot.

Mooring winches
Thick cables or hawsers are used to moor the ship against its platform or terminal. They are pulled in by powerful winches and stored below deck on the voyage.

NEDLLOYD ROUEN

Anchor
The huge anchor is lowered to the sea-bed when the supertanker needs to stay in the same place but cannot moor or tie up. The thrusters and main screws may also be used to keep the ship still or 'on station'.

Thrusters
These small propellers or screws in the side of the hull make the boat swing sideways to help with steering.

Valves
The oil is pumped on and off through connectors. Valves inside make sure it flows the correct way.

58